WHISPERINGS

Dr Gregory Elayadom

First Published in November 2021

ISBN: 978-93-5472-573-9

BLUEROSE PUBLISHERS

www.bluerosepublishers.com

info@bluerosepublishers.com

+91 8882 898 898

Cover Design:

Archita Kumari

Birgit RoBler-Grassotti

Typographic Design:

Ilma Mirza

Distributed by: BlueRose, Amazon, Flipkart

Dedication

This Anthology is dedicated with gratitude and affection to the loving memory of my parents Mary and Scaria Elayadom and the Pioneering Benedictine Fathers of St. Joseph's Monastery, Makkiyad, Wayanad, Kerala, who taught me the love of Nature and humankind.

Acknowledgements

Spirit Divine, I lift up my heart to you for placing me in the midst of misty mountains, wild hanging woods, emerald coloured paddy fields, lakes, islands and where the river Kabini flows singing the agony and ecstasy of the people of Wayanad and while Mother Nature weaves a carpet of many splendoured beauty of a thousand rainbows.

Visually impaired, Dr. S. Suresh Kumar is a renowned Professor of English, critic, creative writer and an eloquent speaker who had helped me throughout our post graduate studies at Nagpur University to open my eyes to what I could not see alone. Thank you dear friend for writing the Foreword to this Anthology.

Dr. Titus, T.K. Professor of English, known for his simplicity, humility and erudition is a creative writer especially, children's books. He is a friend who stood by me through thick and thin and helped me to see the brighter side of human suffering and he always saw a "me" I had not seen. Thank you for writing the Preface for this Collection of Poems.

Credit for the cover photo goes to my friend and acclaimed photographer Birgit Rößler-Grassotti for allowing me to use her photograph of the Lake of Waging in Bavaria. Thank you dear friend for your goodwill and generosity.

I also wish to thank Ms Falguni Dholakia and Mr. Nevin Roy for their goodwill in discerning and typesetting the manuscript.

I thank “BLUE ROSE PUBLISHERS” who went beyond the call of duty to produce a work of quality.

Finally to my wife, Chanda, who stood by me with her presence sometimes more puzzling than beautiful; but, all in all, more beautiful than puzzling.

Dr Gregory Elayadom
P.O. Payyampally
Dist. Wayanad
Kerala, India-670646

About The Author

Dr Gregory Elayadom is a retired professor of English. Widely travelled, Dr Elayadom is a renowned educationist, eloquent speaker who has also worked as a United Nations Volunteer under the aegis of UNDP, in the developing countries of Africa and Bhutan. He has to his credit many poems, articles on education, literature and religion, published.

Dr Elayadom now lives in the beautiful hilly district of Wayanad in the land of "God's own country" Kerala, India.

Preface

Soft, Sweet and Subtle Whisperings

Poetry opens a door to our inner garden allowing us to experience " the bliss of solitude" and leading us to a heightened awareness about our everyday life. Without this awareness, we may not be always able to extract meaning of our experience, and may find ourselves in a situation like the one described by T.S. Eliot in Four Quartets: " We had the experience but missed the meaning".

Poets who throw colour and beauty on the ordinary things of life provide us aesthetic pleasure of the highest kind. Poetry as an art has the power to change the human being from within. And more and more people are turning to poetry for sustenance especially during the times of crisis and inner turmoil. Poetry has the capacity to refresh, humanise and sensitise the readers, perhaps more than any other art form.

This anthology of poetry by Dr. Gregory Elyadom aptly titled as Whisperings bears an eloquent testimony to the above mentioned observations on poetry. The poems in this collection are gentle and graceful whisperings of a poet who has felt deeply and reflected profoundly on life, nature and the world. These poems definitely take the readers on the path of transformation of the heart and offer them a splendid opportunity to contemplate on the profound meaningfulness of life. Here is also a highly desirable and joyous escape route from the mundanity of day-to-day routine.

The poet's ability to absorb the splendour and sublimity of the green wonders of nature and express it through memorable and magnificent words and phrases shines through the entire book. The crystalline images and metaphors used by the poet to clothe natural beauty uplift and liberate the readers. The lines below are self-revealing:

The road paralleled the river flowing

so gently

emeraldcoloured paddy fields on

either side.

vanishing farms and the road

narrows

and turns into a narrow track

and soon the mountain begins to

loom

against the distant horizon

where the dawn lends a pearly tint

to the east.

Who does not wish to travel on such a road by listening to the whisper of the flowing river, gazing at the emerald hued paddy fields, and gradually expanding the horizons of imagination? The poet's ability to draw inspiration and strength from the simple and ordinary things of everyday life is amazing. The following lines are from "Vibrations":

Droplets drumming a quick rhythm

against the leaves

my fears and worries vanished

into the welcoming sunlight

of a warm breeze carrying the

scents

of a golden air filled with a beautiful

dawn.

The river Kabini flowing through Wayanad has a strong influence on the poet. Its music which moves and mesmerises him beyond words follows him everywhere and it "refreshes, renews and revives" his drooping spirits. The river is also a powerful metaphor. In "Climbing Down " he speaks of " The river of life gently caressing dreams, at times flooding with its destructive fury". I cannot resist the temptation here to quote a line from T.S.Eliot's *The Waste Land*.

"Sweet Thames, run softly till I end my song".

The poet's philosophical reflections on the meaning, purpose and also on its unfathomable mystery are undoubtedly profound. He deftly delves into Greek mythology, Indian epics and the Bible to gather the distilled wisdom of the past.

The poet's feeling heart listens to "the agonising sound of human suffering from the neighbourhood". He is stridently opposed to sectarian prejudices, political opportunism and injustice. His heart goes out to the farmers who toil hard but live in dire straits. The saga of hard working migrant labourers causes ripples of anguish in his mental lake. He dreams of a country, " a soft baby-blue meadow", and wants everyone to work unitedly for the common good as the ants who are "all working together to build a sand empire". These ants work “without worrying what would happen if the rains come". The poet's robust optimism and his expectations "for a better morrow, hoping to throw a blanket of love around" are all very promising, especially during these pandemic times of loss, sorrow and deprivation.

The poet's use of fresh and original figures of speech also needs a mention here. At times he surprises and even shocks the readers with his striking images. The opening lines of the poem "Disillusioned" will exemplify this.

Childhood memories all covered by

dust,

some of them like the candle sticks

at the tomb of my parents.

Dr. Gregory is a poet of moral insights. His profound regard for nature, nostalgic love of childhood and shining humanity will strike the right chord with the readers.

Although his poetry is often anchored in the Wayanad landscape, it is never insular but looks beyond the regional to the wider world. His soft, sweet and subtle whisperings will resonate with all kinds of readers. They prompt us to listen to the wind whispering through the woods and to look at the dew drops hanging on the morning grass and also to ponder over the profound mystery of life. As the author memorably says "It takes real struggle to see what life is, a glimpse into myself, a whisper that knows me not." I am looking forward to the next anthology of Dr. Gregory Elyadom.

Ramapuram

Dr.T.K.Titus

28-09-2021

Foreword

Poetry of Admiration and Anguish

Poetry is born when something in nature, society or personal life evokes an aesthetic response or arouses a powerful emotion in a sensitive soul. In "The Figure a Poem Makes" Frost holds that "A poem begins in delight and ends in wisdom." Does it hold good in the case of the poems in this collection? Well, it is for the critics to answer who stand as interpreters between the writer and the reader explaining the one to the other. Arnold, for one, would like poetry to be a "criticism of life". Frost, for his part, would define it as "a clarification of life," although what they mean is not seen to be different in the ultimate analysis.

Most of the poems here, I am sure, will attract the attention of the reader through their pictorial language replete with striking images. As you delve deeper into the experiences behind them, they could be seen moving from the simple to the complex plane altering your configurations of life in the postmodern context. When the poet turns away from the chaotic events in contemporary life and admires the beauty of nature, you see what Frost calls "a momentary stay against confusion." What he observes results in recollection and recollection in turn leads to reflection and what is pondered over finds spontaneous expression, as Wordsworth's *Preface to Lyrical Ballads* explicates it.

Poems generally get written not merely because they profoundly move their writers to admiration or anguish but primarily because of an urge to share their experience with kindred souls. Poems appeal to your head or heart essentially because what they say come out of basic human situations. You recognize in them your own thoughts and feelings even when a poet draws on purely personal experiences. They rise to become truly literary output when they impart artistic pleasure or intellectual profit through rhythmic harmony with vivid images, moving metaphors and other literary and stylistic devices.

Dr. Gregory could be visualized leaning over to whisper to the reader here his profound musings on the fantastic scenery in his home district, distressful scenes of suffering and disenchantments which leave him deeply distrustful of the corridors of power. This reader's comments on most of the poems have been made in the course of their being read casually in the space of a few solitary hours. It hardly needs to be said how interpretations of poems differ from one reader to another and how meanings are seen or created by each reader. In some of the poems you are shown how poetry is produced for its own sake. In some others he shares with you his concerns about certain issues that trouble him. The poet is acutely aware of current social events and cultural clashes and the responses of the powers that be. He touches on them in a sadly satirical tone modulated with moral indignation. What sets him apart from poets who are up in arms against the current order is his awareness of the futility and transience of human struggles to build an egalitarian community without barriers of any kind.

The first poem is indeed a painting of the "Beauty of Nature" as the title defines it. Most of us in the academia are familiar with Plutarch's comment that "Painting is silent poetry, and poetry is painting that speaks." The way the poem here is painted with words reminds you of Pre-Raphaelite poets. You see here a poet reminiscent of D.G. Rossetti with a gift for description of lovely scenes and a propensity for pensive introspection. The reader is delighted by the melody of his verse which at times is Tennysonian. The dominant mood of his poetic output is a dreamy melancholy. The "endless ripples of ecstasy" before long turn into anguish in the next poem, "Whisperings" when the speaker looks "moodily out of the window to the descending eerie silence / thinking of people with their naked ambitions / and steamy hatreds with no lighthouse of hope." In "Directionless" you find "a world more interested in appearance than fact / a people willing to give up love, family, integrity to get to the top." In "Vibrations" one can see his inclination to brood over human greed which leaves nature denuded and how "the weary / Mother would wreak vengeance / upon her mindless prodigal children."

Bafflingly mysterious indeed is what the poet means to say in the poem which would leave a dilettante "Clueless". Does it give you a peep into a dystopian state? "Disconnected Images" again paints the beauty of nature on one side and "the floods and destructive fury of nature" on the other. The rainy season of the hilly district and the ethos of its people are seen here. You see in it their culture of "caring and sharing" but when you get better acquainted with them you see how they "value profit over people / all acting roles instead of acting the way we feel." The title of the seventh poem is suggestive of the writer's return to his sleepy home district after a long interval of life in cosmopolitan cities. His mind runs "in circles" and he worries "about things" beyond his control. When Covid breaks out, he feels "Sequestered in the social wilderness of Corona." One can discern the pressure he feels "to slip into the fog and shadow of Wayanad" with the "vivid chapters" of his life lying already behind him "like a world of mirage." You are made to feel the alienation he experiences "among strange faces / that would neither know nor judge" him. He feels how his old friends will find him "strange and distant."

"Lost Dreams" portrays a perplexed mind in the midst of what the speaker phrases as "Images mingling and confusing / my sense of self" which has "become fragile / scattered across ages of fragmentary memory". What leaves the speaker disturbed is division of society on lines of "caste, creed, and region." What gets depicted in the next poem is the scenic landscape of Wayanad which the poet sees and savours as he saunders along the road that he says "paralleled the river flowing so gently...". The references in "Unsettled Mind" to Iphigenia, Orpheus and Eurydice bring out the poet's insight into Greek mythology. The title is indicative of how deeply the mind of the speaker is churned during the ruminations which lead him to wonder whether he is "in the company / of Iphigenia's ghost".

"Climbing Down" is an exquisitely penned poem conceived in a Wordsworthian or rather Keatsian heart and composed with Arnoldian melancholy. The very first line gives you a foretaste of the poetic beauty mingling with the pathos of life that the rest of the lines are suffused with, “The river of life gently caressing my dreams”. There is no better way of appreciating it than by feeling the poignancy behind each felicitously culled word colouring the pictorial lines. The scenes of suffering uncovered by “Corona” are laid bare again in “Loneliness and Longings” with the mountain forming the background. The poet sometimes seems to hobnob with philosophers like Schopenhauer and tend to conclude that we are born only to suffer, endure and be silent, which “the bitter deaths of a lingering Corona” confirm. Helpless, the poet watches again with “Silent Sighs” scenes of “Death and destruction all around” when Covid claims “thousands”. What draws the ire of the poet is “busy electioneering and swearing in / while lakhs in agony struggle to breathe”.

In “The New Princely Class” you see him having a dig at politicians who feed the poor on “empty promises” which are no more than “soulless bodies”. How poignantly the poem mirrors the misery of the homeless, penniless and hapless man ditched by the world when youth and usefulness bid him farewell and sickness and sorrow wait to see the end! How sarcastic is the concluding line, “costly everything save human life.” To read some of the poems in this collection is to see the painful experiences of the poor, the lowly and the lost which “flash upon the inward eye” of the poet. In “Farmer Friends” one pauses to reflect on the imprecatory words of the Creator of the world, “Because of what you have done, the ground will be under a curse. You will have to work hard all your life to make it produce enough food for you.... You will have to work hard and sweat to make the soil produce anything until you go back to the soil from which you were formed."

"Rustlings" is a lovely poem which gives the reader a glimpse of the scenic beauty of the land that the perennial Kabini flows through but the pain of the poor punctures the momentary pleasure derived from the "sweet songs rocking" the poet "to sleep". The modernist Ezekiel in the poet eclipses the Wordsworthian aesthete. "Aging" shows you how a thinker feels in the evening of life when time has furrowed him with anxiety and angst causing him "to navigate through / the tangled mess of loss and longing." Life's delights disappear with youth leaving most of us to grieve with Coleridge, "Youth's no longer here! / O Youth! for years so many and sweet, / "Tis known, that Thou and I were one".

One could see what "An Agitated Mind" the speaker has on observing national or global events unfolding the way they do, but it is this reader's take that there is lack of tolerance in every land. The question is has tolerance ever been translated into political or religious reality in any part of the globe? E.M. Forster in an essay talks persuasively of the need for tolerance rather than love. We have all been dreaming of both these virtues which continue to be at a discount. One's agitated mind gets compared to boiling water. In the case of water there is return to its original state of tranquillity once its heat disappears. But can the human mind return to its prelapsarian Eden of ease and innocence? Enlightened minds have throughout had utopian "Longings" but one finally listens to the words of the "Mother" seen "In a

Trance", "the Mountain never belongs to anyone / we all belong to the Mountain." The human spirit always triumphs over adversity. "A man can be destroyed but not defeated," as Hemingway puts it. "Struggle" begins with the depiction of a lovely day but the pessimist lurking behind the lover of nature could be seen emerging to point to "the futility of human struggle / in a senseless world: theatre of the absurd."

"Cross, the Symbol of Reversal" is more than a doxological paean to Christ since there is more in it than meets the eye for the reader who goes in for a reading between the lines. You fail at times to empathize with the poet as he paints only his own homeland as "no more" the land of his "dreams" where "tolerance" is "no more a virtue to be cherished." "Haggard" is more political than poetic as it gives obvious expression to the mythical fear of the minority with the Bible-based question at the end, "will you ever cast me out from home, like Hagar / and be condemned to be an eternal wanderer like Ishmael?" In "Fantasy" the poet is reminded of the adage that "eternal vigilance is the price of freedom" and of the warning that servitude will replace it if it is not jealously safeguarded. But some readers are likely to recall Rousseau's words, "Man is born free but everywhere he is in chains."

The muse of the poet beautifully smiles on him as he pens again a pictorial poem with fascinating images in "Haunting Melody". "Melancholy melody" can be seen "spreading across" the speaker's "life" as he watches the "passing scenery" in nature's autumn which is symbolic of human life's decline and fall. He pauses to wonder,

"Am I a mistake of no consequence?" "Dream and Reality" uncovers the wide gulf between the two. It seems to have autobiographical undertones with reverberations of Covid in the background and the gloomy prospect of life's evening coming on. "Refuge" reads like the poem written by a terrified woman on the return of the Taliban in Afghanistan who recently recited some of her lines when she spoke on the BBC. The poem titled "Death" puts you in mind of what Job in the Bible says when he feels devastated, "There is hope for a tree that has been cut down; it can come back to life and sprout.... But a man dies, and that is the end of him; he dies, and where is he then?"

As you read "Wilderness" you go back in memory to the modernist masterpiece, "The Waste Land", where the poet draws on a collage of literary, religious, musical, historical and popular cultural allusions to portray the terror, futility and alienation experienced by humans in the aftermath of the first World War.

The aesthete in the visitor to Salt Lake City is bewitched by the pristine beauty of "Shoreland of Salt Lake" where "nature breathes and throbs / as the migratory bird flaps". The psalmist in him instinctively gives "thanks and praise to the Lord of the Universe" but the environmentalist, bows "to those with great vision / for preserving this nature's fusion / for posterity with so much devotion" and ends the piece with a note of caution, "let no soul this stillness defile / as this silence of eternity prevails." "Waiting to Rediscover" speaks of human aspiration for a "borderless world" or an ideal social organisation or an ideal commonwealth like

Pantisocracy with no divisions of caste or creed that Coleridge and Southey dreamt of in the modern world as philosophers of old did since the days of Plato. One can see the poet ruminating like Thoreau by his Walden Pond, "Far away from the distracted urban life / In a remote hilly village in Wayanad / Where even the wind moves without a sound / And I feel an inner peace never experienced." Like this American poet the writer here returns to the workaday world seeing that "life is a big struggle / And a continual war against destiny".

A reader brought up in rustic surroundings with love of nature, when forced by circumstances to be an urbanite, would pause at times to indulge in "Wistful Thinking", "From this concrete jungle I see no moon or stars / The oppressing air of this jungle will never feel / The cool breeze of my" rustic "home". The lovely lines here, "If only I could mix the soulful melody of the skylark / With the mournful song of the nightingale / I would unravel the mystery of the Universe /And the world will feel my living verse!" recapture the Coleridgean yearning expressed in these lines, "Could I revive within me / Her symphony and song, / To such a deep delight 'twould win me, / That with music loud and long, / I would build that dome in air". The bitter realities of life in the modern world at times seem to leave the poet distraught with his patience running out in poems like "Sleep My Friends, Sleep..." or "Lingering Doubt" with questions which he is unable to answer. In those moments he says, "My mind no more hears the poetry of the wild / or feel the wide open look of the child." "Time to Change" is more political in tone and less poetic.

"Random Sparks" is one of the loveliest poems which needs to be grouped with the one titled "Beauty of Nature". How true it rings as the poet writes, "After a while, love becomes pain" since it "never realizes in real life." Nature alone seems to be your "eternal lover," as he puts it in an elegy. "Nature's unbridled blessings" turn the earth into a paradisal place, but experiences in a world where love fails to flower turns it into a purgatory, if not an inferno. In "Snow Fall" the poet sees "Frost" coming alive on a "cold evening" with his memorable lines, "I have promises to keep / and miles to go before I sleep...." But the writer turns away from the beauty of nature to look at politicians who make promises mostly to break them. All the painful experiences in life seem to flock together to culminate in an intensity of inexpressible grief which finds the speaker in "That numbed disbelief / refusing to dissolve into the sea of sorrow." The words of a poem seldom equal the experience of the poet which underpins them. The experience here is elegiacally titled "Numb Silence". "I am Weary" makes this reader remember the three words which Keats uses to sum up human misery, "The weariness, the fever, and the fret / Here, where men sit and hear each other groan". The last line, "Strike, strike at the root of our callousness" calls to mind Tagore's line, "strike, / strike at the root of penury in my heart." How beautifully the collection is rounded off with the poem, "When Age Carries me...", where universal dissolution happens bringing on "the timelessness, / Where constant flux of time ceases" and "In silence the dear ones share their" sorrows with "the Master Craftsman of the universe / In whom millions place their trust"! The

Artist of the universe is back "once again painting the skies / Lakes, mountains, meadows and streams."

The Gregorian anguish that most of the lines resonate with finds expression like the sobbing wind that plays "Upon the strings of this Aeolian lute" in "Dejection: An Ode". These deeply felt and powerfully expressed poetic "Whisperings" will, no doubt, find an echo in the heart of every reader who has literary sensibility and sees the reality of literature as "a vital record of what men have seen in life, what they have experienced of it, what they have thought and felt about those aspects of it which have the most immediate and enduring interest for all of us," to quote the words of W.H. Hudson.

02.10.2021
Dr. S. Suresh Kumar,

Nagercoil

Table of Content

A Collection of Poems

Beauty of Nature

The morning mist the sun burns away
casting its golden hue of light through the trees
and chirping of birds fill the air;
shadows dapple turning vegetation
a patchwork quilt of light and dark.
The sun sparkling through deep green trees
and the blue of the lake, the green of the valley.
Hundreds of feet below, hillocks
stretched out in a flat and endless plain
before meeting the sky and carry the eye
back through a series of high white clouds.
To the west the descending sun paints
a black glow of trees deep blue then orange
then a creamy yellow while the silence
of woods engulfing me; time suspended
and I feel an eternity elapsing
experiencing the joy and peace
as the sun descends behind the mountain
and like a parting gift wraps the valley with a ribbon
of fire and clothes Wayanad in its innocent glory
and the sight filling my thoughts during the day
and occupying dreams at night
bringing endless ripples of ecstasy.

Whisperings

The reflection of the evening light disappears

in the mirrored glass windows

and a pink sunset streaming through the glass

the cumulus clouds below and show a terrain of deepest green.

Struggling to still my churning thoughts

in the black recesses of the mind with coughs of thunder

this enchanting place with its stunning landscape

I stare moodily out of the window to the descending eerie silence

thinking of people with their naked ambitions

and steamy hatreds with no light house of hope.

The scurrying ants each carrying

it's speck of sand with blind faith

in the seriousness of his mission

all working together to build a sand empire

without worrying what would happen if the rains came.

Gentle rains fall from a cloudless sky

and sheets of water tumbling down the glass.

Watching the progress of the waxing moon

over the hill side and a gust of frigid air

surging in and the sun breaking over the ridge

to the east;

the jot of clouds flowing over the mountain summit

high above its sister mountains

and the plume of vapour singing past;

while the Mother paints all the changes

of the seasons so eloquently showing

the Lord of the seasons and Master of the Universe

and gently leading the world to experience

the *Tao* of the *Chinese*, the *Logos* of the *Greeks*,

the *Jnana* of the *Hindhus* and the *Dharma* of the *Budhists*,
the *Spirit* of the *Christians*

and live in harmony with nature and man

and face the long, long night ahead for the humankind.

Directionless

The agonising sound of human suffering from the neighbourhood

disturbs my peace as the pale glow stains the horizon.

Seeing a people buffeted, trembling and no more certain;

fears, anger, passions and dreads writ large on their faces

as things have become more dangerous with people

desperate to impose ideologies through the barrel of guns

and all human rights violated on the altar of barbaric fanaticism;

gunshots and flowing streams of red staining Mother Earth;

the cry of women and children is like a cry in the wilderness;

their shattered aspirations lie like great monuments fallen

and leaving them to be responsible for themselves

forcing them into the dark recesses of a never ending night.

Around me are people driven by perception

a world more interested in appearance than fact

a people willing to give up love, family, integrity to get to the top.

Paralysed with sadness and unable to rationalise

and infused with a passionate need for justice
I want to cry like a child in my mother's arms
letting all my emotions spit out at her feet and
regain my tranquillity.

Vibrations

Droplets drumming a quick rhythm
against the leaves
my fears and worries vanished
into the welcoming sunlight
of a warm breeze carrying the scents
of a golden air filled with a beautiful dawn.
A sense of euphoria fills my being
and I feel walking into a story, into a legend
into the times of the gods and eternity
and into the shadowed depths of the mountains.
Sitting under the shade of this tree
lost in my reverie of nature;
a sudden thought shakes my body
the thought of the avarice of humankind
disturbing the pulsating, vibrating
nature of it's silence and peace
with their thoughtless behaviour
and of the times when the weary
Mother would wreak vengeance
upon her mindless prodigal children.

Fine tremors go through my body
approaching the only choice we have
when life is cold and blank
on the outside as it would be within
to be terrified and haunted
and to expect the unexpected.
The worst part is no more the fear of death
but the sadness of things that aren't.
A lingering hope what we think true
need not be real or plausible.

Clueless

I see something flare deep in Her cerulean eyes
a spark of pain cool and frosty and a terror raging,
the frustrations and harder emotions;
no refreshing breeze cutting through
the smog and pollution and bitter memories
lingering behind the land sinking
into the rot and mire of a surveillance State
and clueless to what really lurks in the shadows and dark.
Her eyes gleam with shiny unshed tears
staring at with huge blue eyes, the colour of the summer sky;
fascinating, alluring and dangerous
an innate grace and class make her unique
making me wish to chase after her.
Yet the vision of her shattered before I could grasp
and the shards of memories scattering beyond reach
as the River brown with sediments
wound it's sluggish way through the fields
and vanished around the low shoulder of Hill
and the voices and bodies turning into whispers of darkness
haunting the dark moments of sunset and moonrise.

Disconnected Images

I look up to the canopy of leaves above
all of them humming in the rain
watching the wind pass through the trees above;
beneath the mighty sky I sit and brood
seeing a chandelier of yellow street lamps
and the autumnal trees with their yellow leaves
carried off by a gush of wind
seeing my own approaching winter.
The monsoon begins in June
the days become long and longer still.
It rains for days and weeks and months
and I can hardly remember the sun.
Grey smoke of clouds and more chilling rains
the floods and destructive fury of nature;
still there was caring and sharing
and thick warm human relationships.
Nothing is certain, not even the things
one counted on to survive.
Images of past linger on the edge of memory
strange accent and stranger manner of speech.

Here we value profit over people
all acting roles instead of acting the way we feel.
The clouds part to reveal a boundless
range of mountains; the great peak
of Banasura hovering above them all
grand, solemn and unutterably lonely.
It takes real struggle to see what life is
a glimpse into myself, a whisper that knows me not.

Back in My Village

A dazzling sky and a mind running in circles
morning breaks with a dark purple sky
watching the horizon for the rising sun
worrying about things I cannot control.
Sequestered in the social wilderness of Corona
I have to slip into the fog and shadow of Wayanad
and the vivid chapters of my life already
lay behind like a world of mirage.
Henceforth I may live among strange faces
that would neither know nor judge me.
Wayanad this sleepy district of mine
draped in rain and rich foliage
and my old friends finding me strange and distant.
The ruthless pride and pain that keep me so
the reckless ardour that makes me dare
and waver and then again dare
to embrace them as comrades
with capacity for meaningful action
puncturing the inflated sense of my self-worth.
The complex relationships defined by friendship

blood, marriage and immediate geography
succumbing to the voices of avarice, jealousy
pride or cowardice and reflecting
on the brevity and breadth of time-and of life
as I hear someone playing from memory
a piece slow and pensive ; the notes tumbling forth
at uneven cadences and the black birds flapping overhead
fleeting silhouettes against an iron sky.

Lost Dreams

Feeling somewhere else and someone else
as though this familiar country of mine
somehow echoed with the voices of the dead.
I see the people stuttering, mute and helpless
looking at with a silent, concentrated hatred
of a captive watching his enemy
waiting with such a painful endurance
something like a mad defiant gesture.
No moonlight makes its way down
to light the narrow streets of my mind.
Images mingling and confusing
my sense of self has become fragile
scattered across ages of fragmentary memory
years of memory scattered in my mind
a thousand views of my land as tolerant
all embracing, seeking '*Jnana*' and '*Dharma*'
now talons of Ill health pierce its heart
dividing on the line of caste, creed, and region
the horror of which strikes my heart
and the vision of life this great land promised

causing myself dazed and blinking.

My dream of peaceful coexistence

dreamed and then lost the dream

loosing myself in the maze of all these dreams

then staggering out of it back into my own self

seeing not merely a warning but a naked threat

my vision scattering into a tumbling kaleidoscope of images

and my thoughts seemed shattered as well.

Time stretched out and out measureless

without the sun to track across the sky or day glass to turn.

Vanishing Scenery

The flood tide of events that carried me along
had ebbed and left me stranded to make
my way forward by my own strength and will.
The road paralleled the river flowing so gently
emerald coloured paddy fields on either side
vanishing farms, and the road narrows
and turns into a narrow track
and soon the mountain begins to loom
against the distant horizon
where the dawn lends a pearly tint to the east
beyond the dark bulk of the Wayanadan Hills.
The pre dawn breeze so soft and soundless
the moon not quite full lay pale and translucent
low by the eastern horizon.
Honey-gold light of the mid morning
brings strange broken fragments of thoughts
and images sleet through my mind
sharp and glittering as shards of crystal
scattered bits and flashes
that comes like bubbles of light

around the edges of my own memory
giving strange, vivid dreams of lands
I did not know, and voices that murmured
stories of long vanished past,
of people, tired, worried and scared
and the dusty streets crowded on both sides
by the rickety frames of market stalls
at once familiar and strange to me .

Unsettled Mind

I am left in the cool unquiet alone

in the room, flooded with the morning radiance

and the intense churning within

makes me think I am in the company

of Iphigenia's ghost or wondering

what Orpheus's last song

to Eurydice might have been.

A calm suddenly descending on me

as if I were looking at myself from far away, above.

I try to smile; but the expression disintegrate

into the cloying tendrils of childhood receding.

I become more awake as my little village began to twinkle

though the landscape seemed darker, the colours tarnished

I listen to the traffic and the wind

wondering whether I am drowning in my dreams;

the mood grim to the point of suffocation

keeping any sense of lightness at bay.

Slices of light glowing inside the latched shutters of mind;

there are layers here, thousands of years of life and death

and untold history of escape from violence, hunger, disease, famines while I try to understand the nebula that is the end.

The aging night gathering her night skirts

as little drops of perspiration blooming along my forehead

feeling suddenly old like drops of water in a pool

making a little wave and then fade away into nothing.

Climbing Down

The river of life gently caressing my dreams
at times flooding with its destructive fury
and the fear of my own inner chaos
the aching sense that my time is short,
waiting for that eternal silence after death
to read a book in that timelessness of silence.
Thinking of those days and months and years
into which I sorted myself vanishing
like the rounded, frosty puffs of breath
the pain that do not let me cry
yet tears quietly slipping out into thin air
leaving the world all alone to myself
to try to find meaning for life
and the fragrance of memories
of beautiful people and places
of days of contentment and bliss.
Once more I look at the mountain of life
and grow smaller and smaller never reaching
the peak or having any mystical experience to cherish
but only a clear sense of responsibility to a larger world.

Loneliness and Longings

Days laced with terrible loneliness
voices swelling in a sickening wave
sweat trickling down my face.
There is no more the silence of adoration
of the echelons of power or its corridors
only chorus of voices near hospitals
where the air is no more cool and delicious
nor can I hear the muffled roar of music
but only the blurred faces and candles flickering
their rooms filled with mourning sounds
and the mountains echoing in reply
the bitter deaths of a lingering Corona
while the sun wearing down
painting the horizon red and yellow
and my Self divided endlessly
pouring out like a thousand flooding streams
brought by the monsoon rains.
Better to get on the road
to loose myself in the motion
and stop thinking

and see the mountain and beyond
to be lost in the dumbfounded disbelief
of seeing without looking
and feeling without thinking
while they are trapped in a timeless sleep.

Silent Sighs

Floating corpses
Gasping thousands
Missing governments
disgusting sights and agonizing plights
error of judgements
tragedy of mismanagements.
Arms joined in prayer
thousands on funeral pyre
orphaned children
helpless brethren.
Surging bellows of doubts and fears
confusion worst confounded
busy electioneering and swearing in
while lakhs in agony struggle to breathe
vaccination a distant dream
while distressed good-byes scream.
Death and destruction all around
a calmness of graveyard abound
hearts weighed down by sorrow
yet I hope for a better morrow
hoping to throw a blanket of love around
and fill the hearts with peace.

The New Princely Class

Muddy was the path and the clouds dark
with no silver lining, and empty the park.
Alone he came, weary after a long walk
meditating on his fate and futile talk.
Tired, he sat on the leaves decaying
and the yellow leaves dying.
The grand trunk he leaned against for support
looked indifferent like many a report.
A bruised leg, a naked body about to fade
he wondered why God him so wretched made?
Forsaken, helpless and weary, he slept
the stomach rebelled and in sleep he wept.
The falling tears looking like a translucent glass
showing clearly the "New Princely Class."
He saw their sumptuous tables set
and they looked like an ostrich in a net.
His weary hand lean and long
suddenly rose and hit the air strong
as he remembered their empty promises
that looked like soulless bodies after demises.

Waking, he sees his body leeches pestered
like vultures around dead bodies gathered.
"In days bygone you sucked and relieved pain
now suck, suck and leave me slain."
With the sweep of his hands he plucked them one by one
for he was reminded of the promises undone.
Old, poor, naked and weary, he started bleeding,
half dead he saw the leeches greedily swimming
through the blood he shed for living
for well, he knew, for life he was dying.
Slowly he fell and some words came stumbling
this life...wretches living...monument everlasting...
Breathed he, his last, over is his strife,
costly everything save human life.

Farmer Friends

For me the road twists and climbs to higher ground
and I hope to talk of myriad stories of people
both lost and recorded, to my grand children.
Stories of people passing their days in a haze of murky sadness
the agony of sleepless visions and long ticking
nightmare of unquenchable thirst and chills and fatigue
and the dreams of things that will never come back
with its melody unrushed and unfamiliar
creating dark and deep furrows on their brows
and the rain drumming away at their village huts.
They leave their homes before dawn and return after dusk
yet their toil and sweat inadequate to pay their debts.
Their problems never addressed or solved
and are left with the unfortunate human desire
to kick the can of meaning further down an endless road.
The result of their dreams and distance,
the dread and dizziness like a melody drifting off
into hums and moans which no politician can grasp
as they only wish the ensnarement of the masses to thrive

and I can't shake the feeling they are doomed no matter what.

Years of exploitation and oppression resulting

in physical and psychological damage

and their dark mornings, sweaty afternoons and weepy nights;

the poor farmers living in their own private cells

of untranslatable despair, loneliness and neglect

and the last red flash of the setting sun, then cease altogether.

I sit on the banks of Kabini that never runs dry
but refreshes, renews and revives the drooping
spirit of the people of Wayanad and losing myself
to all that would disturb and distract and withdrawing
to the inner sanctuary of my heart to find myself.
I appreciate the descend of the dusk
and the great beauty of the wild around.
The breathtaking scenes of Wayanad
soothing the atmosphere of this backward
district of Kerala, nestling in the splendour
of nature's unalloyed beauty.
I listen to the silent stirrings and whispering
responding to the genial generosity
of the inner inspirations and explore
the depths of interior solitude and silence
and hear the constant and tranquil
sound of the ever-flowing waters.
I enjoy the quiet moonlight view
the breeze filtered through,
causing the leaves to clasp gently.

The hills around me sing
sweet songs rocking me to sleep.
I dream politicians taking advantage
of every tear that falls from the suffering
eyes of the poor, the nameless multitude
and the people screaming and hating one another
and I wake up sighing and groaning
and feeling lost in time, in my reverie
like a bird which cannot live
in a cage and who cannot be free.

Aging....

The nagging, incessant feeling
that something is terribly wrong;
hyper awareness or heightened sensitivity?
the rush of grief that would
spill out of the tiniest crack.
The sharp and agile mind
slowly becoming senile.
Dreaming of life in my home
growing old, content, so at peace
life still full and textured.
Yet worrying how many years left of sanity
I fall asleep picturing my mother's smile.
My heart beating wildly
pounding against my chest
feeling a wave of dread
something like terror as I imagine
the next years of my journey
that I have to navigate through
the tangled mess of loss and longing.
Almost in pain I go through

all the beautiful old landmarks
that had been demolished in my life.
I long to preserve the fleeting past
not knowing what I would be able
to hold on to and what would disappear.
As evening leaned towards darkness
I watch the sun sink into the sky.
weighed down by my own feelings
I descend into deeper unknowns
powdering the reasons that elude
but to which I remain surely tied.

An Agitated Mind

Learning to swallow the uncomfortable feeling
and the fear and lack of courage
to be carried off into peaceful dreams;
the shadowy presence eliciting
continual passion and hopelessness
and feeling a stranger in my own land
I wander off in solitary walks
a menacing alien and apart
and long for that Eden that never
extended beyond childhood reverie.
I see a procession of limbs and wheels
all fighting for space in the scorching sun
and frightened to voice their new found fear
of the present dispensation where
the core values cherished by our fore fathers
are thrown to the winds for their narrow gains.
They have lost their willingness
to work together towards common good
and their promise of another life
warm, sensual, exotic and all embracing

lay bare like a shattered landscape.
Foolish of me to have taught to have faith
in other people, not Hindu or Muslim or Christian
to be cooperative not competitive
freedom to disagree without rancour;
I am frightened at the difference caste
money and religion made in my land;
at times even the lingering hope frightens me.
I long for the politicians to speak words
carrying message, support an idea
words that transform showing right and wrong
between dignity and servitude
between commitment and indifference.
But I see only confusion and anger
shaping the destiny of the young.
I wish to sit silent listening to the traffic
trying to retell an old story in a distant voice
as the tolerant India lay behind me
like a childhood dream, never to come back.

Longings

Twilight twists like light
refracted through a prism
showing a scattering of colourless houses
and people roaming aimlessly
as the moody cloud cover clears.
The river flows with the melodic certainty
of a heartbeat that is becoming weary
as the bond between the farmer and soil
is lost as as nature's protection fail.
I long for a vibrant and varied
political culture wherein every
taxpayer and farmer has a stake
In a generous welfare State.
A fertile ground for creative imagination
not a victim of its own success.
Now everything seems totally out of proportion
waiting for a sun that changes the colour of everything.
A feeling of never ending confusion
replaces the feeling of tranquil life.
Yet I dream of my country

not a threatening roaring monster

but a soft baby-blue meadow

warm and welcoming like a mother

nurturing possibilities never before imagined

where journey of mind, body and spirit

rich in self discovery , exploring

the surrounding to find a place

within every one and have a lasting

personal enrichment and bliss

and bring the dramatic landscapes alive.

driving away the darkness before

and an empty heaven above

making every one believe his country

to be the most beautiful in the world.

In A Trance

It is harder now to capture
the harmony of sounds
their rhythm, their cadence;
feeling adrift in a raging sea
in the middle of the night,
floating into nothingness
beyond time and space.
Images appear as blurred
recollection of memory,
experiencing a mixed feeling
of shame and anger breaking
free from the shackles of time
at the hundreds of furrows
ploughed in through rough skin
and the obstinate silence of authorities
their sighs and groans
too deep for words, Oh! Mother.
I hear the enchanting words
of Mother transporting me
to another country and another time

where love never sets

and compassion never dries up

and I loose myself in them

and hear her whisper

the Mountain never belongs to any one

We all belong to the Mountain.

Struggle

There is something beautiful
in its nearly silent emptiness
the beautiful day, the sky
in a single stretch of blue
untouched by clouds
the sun gleaming and bright.
Yet a wave of sadness
filling my veins as I watch
mothers struggling to be attentive
attuned to the moods and needs
of cherished moments of togetherness
sweating in the oppressive heat
reminding the futility of human struggle
in a senseless world: theatre of the absurd.
You just cannot buy love
like you buy your groceries.
Confident and humble
emotionally astute, we still need
the stories of the enslaved and under privileged
and avoid confronting uncomfortable

painful truth breaking my heart
each time I see their relentless struggle
against the horrible crippling
depression that envelops
the flicker of hope and euphoria
and a whole vile economy teeming
under the surface of Indian domestic life
like truth often filed away in catalogues
filed into oblivion as truth never makes news.

Cross, The Symbol of Reversal

Symbol of gruesome and painful execution
Repulsive public display of human agony
Symbol of divine curse on the executed
Symbol of ignominy, symbol of hopelessness.
Cross of Christ that changed the world and symbol
Symbol of triumph over death by the cross
Symbol of atonement, symbol most powerful
Instrument of salvation, symbol of glory.
The power of a vision of hope
Even in the encircling suffering
Christ the good Samaritan died on the cross
Assuring in inversion of contemporary value system
Compelling symbol of reversal
Symbol of power in powerlessness
Symbol of life in death
The uniqueness of His suffering on the cross
Symbol of reversal and triumph over death.
Symbol that works on many levels
Symbol that transforms with new meaning
Symbol that opens universal dimension.

Symbol of supreme sacrificial death

Symbol of ransoming and redeeming

Symbol of the vicarious suffering

Of Christ the innocent victim

Disillusioned

Childhood memories all covered by dust
some of them like the candle stick at the tomb of my parents.
Frightened by my own growing shadow
and the long journey to unknown places
where I will lose my ability to pretend
and the mind able to see beyond the horizon
where there shall be no conspiracy of silence
or hiding the culpability of violence
and complete freedom from predators.
My mind the multicoloured painting
fades as I drift away to the haunting
curtain that is falling on this land of mine.
My mind is now gripped by a sense of fear
as dissenting voice brutally silenced
and dissenting Indians labelled antinational
and young students mercilessly attacked
and communal violence so frightening.
This is no more the India of my dreams
and tolerance no more a virtue to be cherished.
Temples of learning have turned into battle fields

as goons on rampage at college campuses.
Weep my Mother weep, weep for your children dear
for they have lost their equilibrium.
The growing age has made me weak
and the mindless violence forces me to seek
a safe passage from this land of chaos
to a land of eternal Spring and tranquillity.

Haggard

Mother dear, I feel like one tempest tossed
the fear of drowning grips like one possessed
and the stream of my consciousness falls
into the depth of unfathomable chaos
of confusion worst confounded in the wilderness
as the destiny of your children hangs in the interpretation
of our revered Constitution by the Law makers
as this country of mine becoming a jungle
of sadism, perversion and violence.
Both the mystic believer and the indifferent atheist
hope all the pain will be washed away by time.
And I love to walk free with my thoughts and longings
and nourish my country with my blood if needs be
while longing for the exquisite peaceful vista of India.
Mother, prices roaring, inflation rising
embarrassing mismanagement of economy
employment opportunities so scarce
frustration writ large on the faces of the youth
and their muffled voices breaking loose
as the surging billows of rising doubts and fears

beset the Nation like never before.
Mother dear I love my country reach the height of the sky
a living example of unity in diversity
where different cultures, traditions and religions
meet and mix resulting in constructive reactions
and discrimination thrives not in the peoples' minds.
Mother will you ever cast me out from home, like Hagar
and condemned to be an eternal wanderer like Ismail???

Fantasy

This sick sinking feeling within
prevents the soothing sound of wind
or the cool crisp breeze filter in to the mind
though craving to take deep breath
savouring the sweetness of it .
There is tension in the air
a sense of something waiting to happen
as the low rhythmic, tuneless hum
that is filling the mind so oppressive.
I see the people with their faces twisted
with pain and tears and caught
between the instincts of fight and flight,
the impulse to stay or run away
from the real or imagined terrors of darkness.
I see them young and old, mother and children
all protesting in a creative and novel way.
This irrational sense of being watched
make me slip into a sudden lapse
of irrationality impacting my nervous system.
This nagging sense of wrongness some where

fails my struggle to verbalize this sensation.
With a look of long suffering patience
or a confusion deep inside, a hunting
instinct fighting for control.
I have become nothing more than a symbol
for dredged up from the collective unconscious.
To the east the horizon is darkening
and the cold wind ushering in the imminent night
and my voice sounding distant to my own ears
"eternal vigilance is the price of freedom."

Haunting Melody

I watch the passing scenery
A sea of russet gold of autumn leaves
Woven with the fire of oncoming fall
As I walked through the forest.
It seemed familiar, but strange too
A pain too sharp to ignore
And a lightness spreading up to my throat
Making tears blur my vision
A sob erupted with an ugly heave
Am I a mistake of no consequence?
A slow throb of life, a haunting reverberation?
I fondle the rose petals soft against
My finger tips and watch clouds drift around
The scariest thing I could think of
Was no longer existing: True death.
Fire coloured leaves floated
To the ground behind me
As I turn from the garden, heart aching
And my emotions spiralling out of control.
The sweet scent is overwhelming

Fiery petals tickling my nose
The spicy scent so thick I could taste it.
Petals rasped under my finger tips
The scent of roses warmed my senses.
The sun drifted towards the west
Like music from centuries ago.
Melancholy melody spreading across my life
The music gasping, surging with fear
Looming long and low and lonesome
A haunting echo of blossoming youth
And my existence seemed so fleeting.
I arrive at the beach, all sand and frothy
And listening waves brushing sand
Hoping to scribble happiness into my life
And listen to the melody of my friends' voices

Dream and Reality

Far away in a strange alien land

far away from my native Wayanad

where the Kabini flows whispering the struggle and triumph

of the migrant hardworking men and women

and their shared helplessness, agony and ecstasy

where I used to dream of an alternate reality.

As evening drifted into the realm of weariness

and my eyes roll back into darkness

weary through the ether of time

fractured with shadows and ripples

and the wind rustling the leaves on the branches

like flirting with annihilation.

I look at myself and the natural decay of aging

and the cycle of seasons like the traffic light

changing from red to green and yellow again

and then again rhythmically unreeling;

then evoking the lost world of childhood

I plod and ponder and at times persist

seeing the looming shadow of swift decline.

I hear the frightened eerie gasping voices

the helpless lakhs and the monster Corona
our Shiva the destroyer of human vanity.
My mind the labyrinth of time
where people and places come and go
like fleeting series of images
asking are we to be vanquished
defeated by forces unknown??
The time would come sooner
when I would unlikely have the stamina
or the time to say "Thank You" for loving me.
Andrew, my little grandson curls up beside
bringing me back to time and reality
and once again I dream not of the past
but of the wide-open future for him.

Families are scattered, hearts broken
waves of pain surging one after another;
and the dark days of terror returns
and the fear drains the beauty of life
as the fabric of a peaceful society
destroyed by a few fundamentalists
and my vision collapsing into
a vacuum of disappointment.
Awaiting a time when I can go
without any checks to where I will
and the freedom to sing like birds
sans any religion, caste or politics
and open the windows of ages
filling my mind with the wisdom of the sages
enabling to read my mind so complex
and give expression to words unspoken for so long.
Playing a delicious melody that scented the wind
under the quivering stillness of the watching trees
as the night shifts her horizon
contemplating the kindling of the dawn

and the damp chill that had settled into night
leading me to Mother Nature's lap
to find meaning of pain, beauty, damnation,
horror and find redemption on her lap
as she sings of a tale of lifelong quest for love.

Death

There are seasons and regenerations
the soil seems to come alive
with grubs and bugs and worms;
birds chirrup and buds swell
and each part of nature burgeons
at its own pace after winters death.
Will I face the last battle of life with death
with tears of regret silently streaming
down the cheeks for the lost part of life
or bravely engage and grapple like
Jacob with the angel compelling the spirit
to bless till this journey is through,
and thank the Giver of life for its gifts
and crush the waves of death
till the breeze turn warm at the end of Winter
and pass the last few days like dreams
ushering harmony and convergence
of illusion and reality in annihilation?
Or feel like a sob welling up my chest
concealing it with a cough into a kerchief

and left alive but incapable of joy or sorrow
in an air filled with heat and dust
withered and paralysed slipping into oblivion
signalling a violent morning about to dawn
and a judgement where mercy reigns over justice?

Wilderness

The critical times hard to deal with
Financial crisis, family breakdowns
Deadly disease outbreaks , wars
Natural and manmade disasters
Terrible betrayal by representatives
Crushing anxieties of new responsibilities
Discovery of life threatening illness
Invisible struggles, the untold pain
The depressed silence, tearing nerves
From where no ray of hope comes
An excessive worrying world
Out of proportion, out of control
A wailing sea of humanity
Never playing a poor hand well
In the stunning vista of wild hills and glens
My mind in a shattered landscape
and blink in the harsh sunlight

Shore Land of Salt Lake

A heavenly indefinable joy fills
as the sights and sound fills
my heart on the great shore land
of the enchanting Salt Lake City.

The nature breathes and throbs
as the migratory bird flaps
my mind takes a flight
and merge into the living nature
giving thanks and praise to the Lord of the Universe.

In the seemingly endless expanse
of mountains on all sides
clouds drifting across the skies
catching and tangling on peaks
while gentle breeze stirring the waves
I gaze towards the mountains
that rise like distant walls
protecting the Salt Lake city.

Beauty captures me in a moment
changing me forever in this enchantment.
feel secured in this vastness
where time stirs not the stillness .

With folded hands I bow to those with great vision
for preserving this natures fusion
for posterity with so much devotion
let no soul this stillness defile
as this silence of eternity prevail.

Waiting to Rediscover

I dream of a rare sight
Of a border-less world
Where merging of cultures
Is complemented
By merging of concerns:
Where people will meet the needs
Of people and live a constructive life.
But
I see people all around me
With tremulous voices
And suppressed pain
A pain that swelled and crashed
And then again swelled
With unimaginable loneliness.
Its enormous size
Of suffering and evil frightens
As religion instead of giving solace
Has become an unfailing cause of strife .
Deep reflection and serious debate
Solves not the enduring questions

Confronting human experience

Baffling me out of my very being.

I try hard to empathize with

A disillusioned world all around

Waiting to rediscover

The Compassion of Christ

The "*Karuna*" of Lord *Budha*

District in Distress

Far away from the distracted urban life
In a remote hilly village in Wayanad
here even the wind moves without a sound
And I feel an inner peace never experienced

But now the desperate cry of the farmers
And the trumpeting of wild tuckers
Disturb this tranquillity with insecurity and fears
As even the monsoon appears to abandon Wayand.

This land of mine a great tourist destination
This landlocked district now engulfed by stagnation
Is a place most backward where the tribals
Still cry for their land and try to keep their customs and rituals.

Yet others plead for connectivity by train and air
And restoring of night travel to states near
As the farmers mourn for the loss of their crops
By the encircling wild life sucking their red drops

And the apathy of powers never heeding to their demands

Lack of powerful voice to empower their minds and hands.

Equal opportunity for people still a distant dream

And through these feeble words their griefs I beam

Telling them again and again, life is a big struggle

And a continual war against destiny the ripple.

Wistful Thinking

Could I travel along the road I liked
Like the rays of the dawn
Knowing I am at the end of the road
And the dusk is in sight, hope lingers!
Could I imbibe the music of the universe
I would explain the mystery of the world
And empathise with the innocent victims
Of man's inhumanity to man and nature.
The retreating melody of the chirping birds
The drying music of the jungle streams
The sighs from the broken families
Welling up my mind as weird dreams.
As the destructive fury of nature fumes,
And the rustling wild hanging woods ever sighs
I long for the unalloyed joy of the joint families
The grand children playing under the mango tress.
The elaborate bath in the limpid waters
Of the river that flows so silently
And long for those days receding to memory;
The moon light caressing the courtyard

The stars playing hide and seek.

From this concrete jungle I see no moon or stars

The oppressing air of this jungle will never feel

The cool breeze of my home in Wayanad.

The mysterious lyric echoes in my ears

As the universe that ever celebrates its life.

The hot black spitting chimney

Never feels nature's pulsating harmony.

If only I could mix the soulful melody of the skylark

With the mournful song of the nightingale

I would unravel the mystery of the Universe

And the world will feel my living verse !!

Sleep My Friends, Sleep...

Sleep my friends, sleep,
Sleep in your cosy little homes
As our brave Jawans bleed.

When will the authorities heed
To the cry of the 'bleeding drops of red'?
On the borders of our country
Witness protests at encounter sights
And school children pelting stones.
A tragedy indeed, the politicians blame each other
Failing to give a unified response loud and clear.

Bleed my country, bleed
At the escalating situation
While the enemy mutilate the bodies
Of Jawans who die that we may live.
I watch helplessly, day by day
The martyrdom of the brave soldiers.

The mutilated bodies of our soldiers
Cry for avenging this despicable act.
Let not their blood go in vain
Lest the country will never forgive
The rulers who fail to give a befitting response
To our enemies playing with our patience.

Lingering Doubt

Dark clouds gathering on the horizon
Farmers praying fore more rains in unison.
Sound of rain drops falling on leaves
Branches of trees shaken by winds
Oh! rains that energize life in nature
And its destructive fury bringing bleak future.

Colleagues who stood by me through thick and thin
All drifted away behind the curtain of death.

My mind no more hears the poetry of the wild
Or feel the wide open look of the child.
Is it a welcome shade or master of surprise
Like calm waters most deceptive to surmise.
I wait for the uncertain time I should face
Oblivious of what lies beneath the surface.
Love to leave this world without being seen
As my day wears on to that lifeless scene.

What is this mystery called death

A gate, the end, or a rebirth

A journey to some subtle region of sorrow or mirth

Pity! I must first die to know what is its depth!!

Time to Change

The waves of enthusiasm for "*Achhe Din*"
and the promise of all inclusive development
turn into disillusion and frustration
like the apple Eve offered Adam before they fell.

I see them in the market and fields
offering neither confidence or conversation.
The broken pieces of their hearts
asking questions that linger deep within.

Their struggle with the uncertainties of life;
their fear and pain and challenge—
Can the tallest statue or changing names
give some clue to what they are about to face?

Their faces look vulnerable and softer
and I try to blend in with the crowd
feeling more deceitful telling the truth
than I would a lie; longing to ask and answer.

Life itself has become a risk.
My vision blurs and voice breaks
caught between fear and anger;
their empty expression and looks
weary in a way I have never seen before.

I feel a fluid state of identity
before the desperation and disorder
of the powerless at the picture-perfect land
flowing with milk and honey
and the frustrating echo of "*Achhe din*"
where I loose my capacity for wonder.

After a while, love becomes pain;
It speaks so much without a word
Like a message that transcends logic
As in me there is nothing that is mine.
I try to define, destroy or drive
And envy rivers flowing unmindful
Of geographical boundaries.

This curtain will surely fall one day
Loneliness, loss, the ups and downs
And love that never realizes in real life.
Beautiful sunshine caresses
Through the cloudless skies
And in dappled sunlight
My imagination flies.
The glorious evening
The sun starting its lazy descend
Shadows lengthening
And dreams and tears fusing
Like fragrance and breeze.

Beauty without boundaries

Nature's unbridled blessings;

Summer at its romantic best

Heaven on earth; but leave I must

Experience that is the truth;

Life a creative process

And we live in a world which we create

And give the soul to recreate.

Snow Fall

I sit by the window watching
the snow fall on this cold evening
and Frost comes alive and his
"I have promises to keep
and miles to go before I sleep...."

It brings to me the unkept promises of politicians
and a vast spectrum of lost horizons.

I look around for the land of the free
and see the faces vulnerable and frightened
come oblivious of the lynching crowd.

Dread and nerve-splitting pain
spilling out of my heart into my chest
lows into my limbs and all the way
to my scalp and down to my feet.

I long for the powerful feelings of love
of hope and trust that made all dreams
possible, attainable and admirable.

Never wanting to get sucked
into the destructive vortex
often created by the rich and the powerful
and seeing the individual rise
and the collective decline of society
I try to unite my many worlds
into a single harmonious whole
and try connecting to that single "caste", Indian
feeling like an explorer fearing danger
in the untouched wilderness.

I look for the pleasure of company
and the joy of human warmth and tolerance
and wait for the trees to sprout
and reach heavenward and the world
feels like a green house giving
people a chance to change and regenerate

Numb Silence

Like parched land awaiting summer rain
I wait for your call every morning invain.
Oh! dear brother do you hear my cry
silencing the voice of reason
coming from the depth of my soul
as your life ebbed away in my hands
and I looked helplessly into your vacant eyes
feeling it in my body, feeling it in my being?
The bruised body, the broken skull
blood flowing like rivulets from ears and nostrils
your violent gasping for breath
was like a dagger piercing my being.
Suddenly a hushed silence
an intense sense of loss
engulfing my being like never before
wanting to dissolve into thin air.
Tears brimming at the brim
refusing to trickle down
as I carry your lifeless body
to the final resting place.

Is it a weird dream or a cruel joke
the feeling of being carried by him
on his shoulders, lifeless I lay
like a bundle to be dumped?
That numbed disbelief
refusing to dissolve into the sea of sorrow.
No mortal gets all the wishes fulfilled
only destined to live 'to die to sleep.'
Clothed in perennial Spring
before the presence of the Mighty King
where the river of life flows uninterrupted;
you call me teasingly
to watch the sun rise again
to play with the eternal lover, the Nature.

(written soon after the accident and death of my younger brother)

I am Weary

Weary of all the rapes and suicides
Frightened womenfolks, frustrated farmers.
Weary of all the rapes on democracy
Weary of all the strikes and loss of property.
Tears trickling down from the deepset eyes
Of farmers crying hopelessly for help.
The unseasonal rains, hailstones thick
Melts not the heavy burden of indebted farmers.
Weary of farmers mindless suicides
And brave officers driven to the dead end.
Weary of representatives wasting precious time
Discussing figures and colour of women.
Weary of their making a mockery
Of the promises so eloquently made
And the aspirations of innocent people.
Weary of calculated attacks on prayer halls
Weary of expressions “we condemn”.
Save us Oh. Lord, from this hopelessness
Strike, strike at the root of our callousness.

When Age Carries Me...

When age carries me on its wings
To the other side of age, the timelessness,
Where constant flux of time ceases
And the mighty powers collide the last time
The combat so deadly in this cauldron
And the streams of compassion dries up.
In silence the dear ones share their sorrow
To the master craftsman of the universe
In whom millions place their trust
The serene breathtaking landscape, the sign of hope.
The rays of the sun sparkle on the waters
And life like the rhythm of the tides
Moves on giving wings to its dreams
Hoping to wake up hearing the chirping of birds
And seeing the artist once again painting the skies
Lakes, mountains, meadows and streams.

www.ingramcontent.com/pod-product-compliance
Ingram Content Group UK Ltd.
Pitfield, Milton Keynes, MK11 3LW, UK
UKHW041820200726
13854UKWH00001BA/141

9 789354 725739